The International Design Library®

AFRICAN DESIGNS OF NIGERIA AND THE CAMEROONS

Caren Caraway

Eshu, I honor you because of your power, *ashe*.
Eshu, you are the road maker.
Come with kindness to me and to my family,
     who serve you with gifts.
Eshu, you are the present giver.
Make me rich and the mother of good children.
Never allow your children misfortune.
Come with your beautiful appearance,
     you son of cowries.

(Adetohun Flemoso B.C. 1972)

Chant of Elemoso, the chief priestess of Eshu,
when she kneels before the shrine.

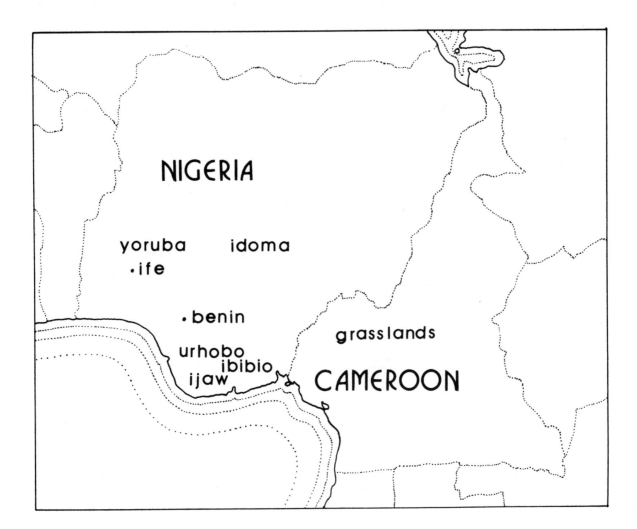

NIGERIA

yoruba   idoma
 •ife

•benin
                    grasslands
urhobo
     ibibio
ijaw   CAMEROON

INTRODUCTION

Africa, earth's second largest continent, is a beautiful land of violent contrasts. Its challenging environment includes some of the world's highest mountains, mightiest rivers and greatest deserts. Inhabiting this land are a great number of peoples of very diverse cultures. Many believe in a concept of a unified whole of the entire cosmos. Man must harmonize with the totality, and in so doing must appease the spiritual force of all that is. This attempt has resulted in the creation of objects to influence spiritual powers. African art is primarily religious. Masks, statues, fetishes and other items are used to placate natural forces, establish connections with those who have died or are to be born, attract good fortune and uphold traditional values. Objects have been made from stone, metal, terra cotta, ivory, leather and wood, but few artifacts carved from wood survive more than a couple of hundred years because of damage by insects and the tropical climate.

Nigeria, Africa's most densely populated country, is located on the Atlantic Coast. It has a swampy coastal region, broad river valleys with tropical rain forest, plateaus of grassland savannas dotted with fire-resistant trees, and thorn woodland that occupies the northern boundary area. Little is known of Nigeria's history before the 15th century, but it has an ancient artistic tradition extending from the 5th century B.C. to the present time. A great variety of politically decentralized tribes have long inhabited Nigeria and created a profusion of art styles. The earliest known works appear to have been produced by a culture that flourished from the middle of the first millenium B.C. until the middle of the first millenium A.D.

The art of BENIN spanned five centuries. It was royal art created by craftsmen organized into guilds, under the patronage of the Oba or King. The people of Benin, known as Bini, claimed descent from the skies and the Oba was considered to rule by divine right. For centuries the Oba maintained predominance over a wide area of Nigeria by military might, and many kinds of artifacts were made to serve the state by symbolizing the Oba's power and prosperity. Early kings encouraged carving of wood and ivory. The Oba was given half of the ivory obtained by any hunter and much of that ivory was carved for his ceremonial apparel. But the most important material used by Benin artists was bronze, and with it they produced the largest amount of sculpture of ancient

Nigeria. Tradition claims that when the Oba died his head was sent 120 miles away to the Holy Yoruba City of Ife for burial. A bronze head was then sent from Ife for placement on his ancestral shrine. Then, in the late 14th century, it was requested that a bronze master be sent from Ife so the Bini could make the commemorative heads themselves. Igueghae taught bronzecasters who were then forbidden by threat of death to produce bronzes for anybody but the Oba. For several centuries, bronze castings and ivory carvings were made with hard steel tools that are a mystery to modern steelmakers. The Bini perfected a method which produced castings of extraordinary thinness and treated the subject matter with relative naturalism. They used their sumptuous castings to decorate a magnificent city. Benin, capital of the Edo-speaking people, was located 75 miles inland from the mouth of the Benin River. Both city and royal palace were protected by ten-foot-high walls. Benin was transversed by thirty broad streets, lined with large, low houses containing many rooms and galleries walled with red polished clay. The splendid palace contained marvelous structures connected by colonnades of wooden pillars that were adorned with bronze plaques glorifying the Oba. Cast from the early 16th century, the plaques were not made after 1700. In the early 19th century the quality of the art deteriorated and traditional Benin art was brought to an end in January of 1897, when two of the Oba's chiefs killed a British consul and most of his party. The British then deposed and exiled the Oba and sent thousands of pieces of art to England.

Located in the rain-forest area, IFE has been the spiritual center of the Yoruba nation for centuries. It was the home of the Yoruba oracle and the One or King, who was considered a descendant of the first Oni, Odudua, one of the gods who descended from heaven, to oversee the creation of earth by sixteen chickens who scratched it up from the sea. The art of Ife ranged between the 11th and 15th centuries and was unique for its idealized naturalistic treatment of human forms. Ife artists created terra cotta heads with fine incisions lining the faces, and full-length human figures. Sophisticated bronze heads were cast by the lost-wax process, as were figures of royal personages and their attendants. Surprisingly, because of the scarcity of stone in the forest regions of Africa, there were also stone carvings. Ife held widespread influence over kingdoms founded by sons of Odudua, but it declined as a political empire in the 16th and 17th centuries.

For hundreds of years the YORUBA have been one of the largest and most prolific art-producing tribes of Black Africa. Since prehistoric times they have lived in the southeast region of the country, where they are divided into twenty autonomous city-states, whose kings claim descent from Odudua, the first Oni of Ife. Yoruba art is dedicated to a pantheon of gods, and is divided into works for the Orisha (demi-god) cults and the large number of secret societies which use them for annual fertility rites, members' funerals, and to frighten women.

Privately owned items are used for divination to forecast daily events, influence decision-making, and foretell what grandparent is returning to life in an expected child. They were also used in the cult of twins, for Yoruba welcomed twins, believing them to be more intelligent and lucky. Twins were considered to share a single soul and if one died, a statue was made to be the dwelling place of the deceased. Present Yoruba artists continue to work with wood, ivory, iron, brass and beads, producing masks, statues, portals, doorposts and ornamental vessels.

The URHOBO live in the swamps and forest of the lower Niger River area. Most of them are devoted to one forest or water spirit, and they have developed a distinctive style of carving, with cubist tendencies, for invocation of the spirit and for mask dances.

The IJAW (IJO) live in the mangrove swamps and jungles of the Niger River Delta, inhabiting palm-rib huts in village clusters that claim descent from a common ancestor. Formerly feared headhunters, they are governed by an assemblage of elders. Secret societies maintain the ancient practices used to affect supernatural activity. Figures and masks, made with animal, human combined with animal or geometric features and worn horizontally, are made to influence the spirits. Non-masked dancers ceremonially over-power masked performers in a symbolic manifestation of man's desire to conquer and control the spirit responsible for floods and fishing, who is so important in lives dependent on water for food and communication. Every twenty-five years the water spirits of the eastern Ijaw are invited to a great banquet in a request for fertility. Fishing and the collection and trade of palm oil are the basis of the Ijaw economy, which formerly was fueled by their active participation in the slave trade.

The IBIBIO are a coastal people inhabiting the Calabar province of southeastern Nigeria, where they practice rain forest cultivation of taro, yams and cassava. The Ibibio live in compounds grouped into village sections. Villages of 100 or 200 people form clans which are united by descent from a single parent village or common tutelary spirit, and have the same culture and language. They are ruled by the powerful Ekpo secret society which honors dead ancestors, enforces the law, and conducts ceremonies to insure community welfare, individual fertility and abundant harvests. One of their great spirits used to demand child sacrifice. The secret societies possess a large number of masks and wooden statues of different style characteristics. Some of the oldest carvings were considered tribal ancestors; others were used as marionettes in plays. Skin-covered heads were produced by some of the Ibibio.

Most of the IDOMA live in the savanna country of northern Nigeria, and most are Moslem. Their social structure is based on land-holding lineages, with a chief presiding over each group of several units. They grow a mixture of savanna and rain-forest crops. Carving of religious objects is only done by small groups of Idomá.

The Federal Republic of Cameroon lies east of Nigeria. Its terrain includes the coastal region, hills, a great rift valley, mountains and plains, and it has a variable tropical climate. Diverse ethnic groups have inhabited the region since prehistoric times. Artists and their creations are highly esteemed, comprising four large style regions. The art of the Northern area is very abstract with no representative features, while that of the Coastal Region has been affected by contact with Europeans. The realistic carved wooden heads of Cross River are covered with skin, recalling times when the former headhunters danced with the heads of their victims tied to their own heads. The prolific artists of the beautiful Grasslands have been influenced by cultures from the north. They work with brass, wood, clay and beads, embellishing nearly every object. Many of the items are boldly decorative royal art and include thrones, palace pillars, vessels, pipes and drums. There are also masks, ancestor cult statues and fetishes, as is typical of so much African art. Each tribe specializes, but there is a uniform style.

C.C.

NIGERIA

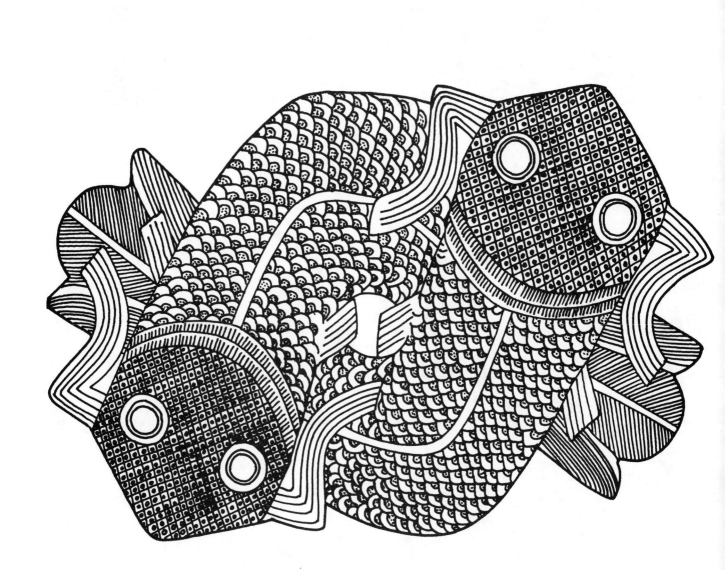

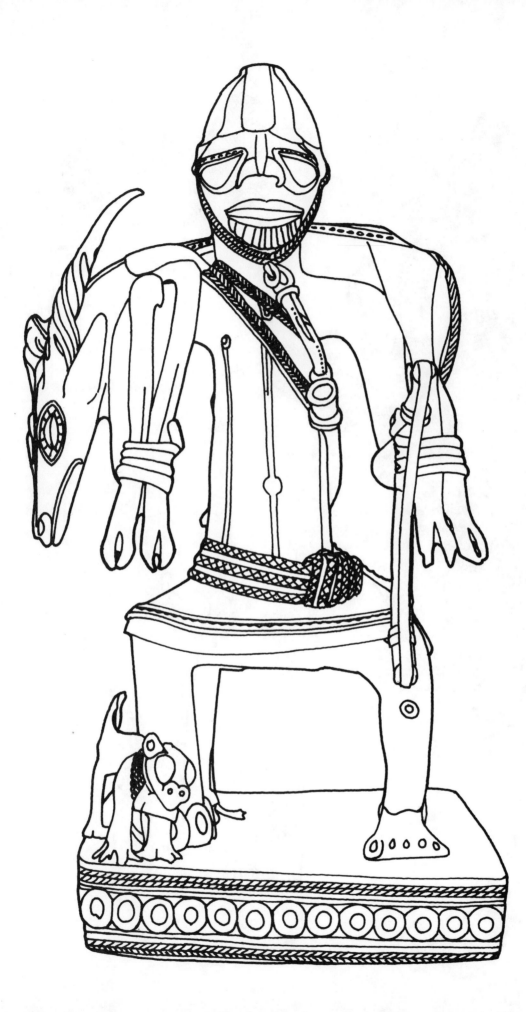

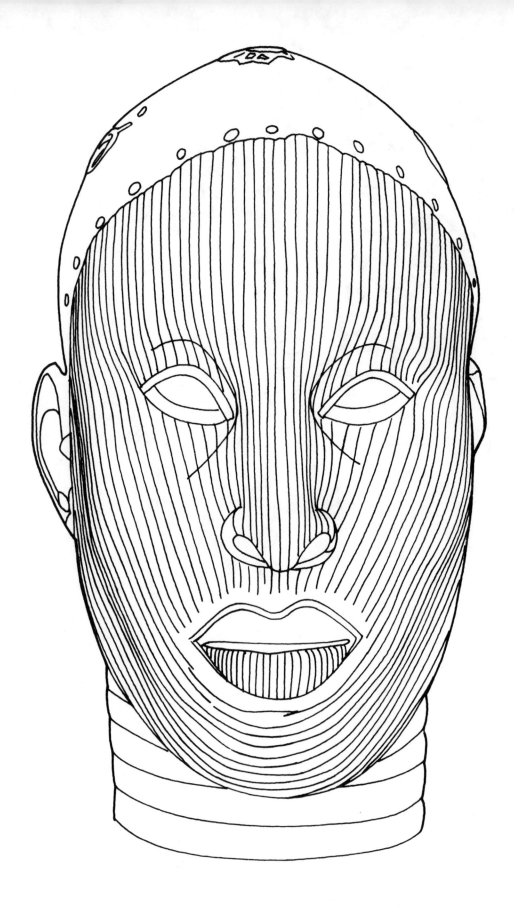

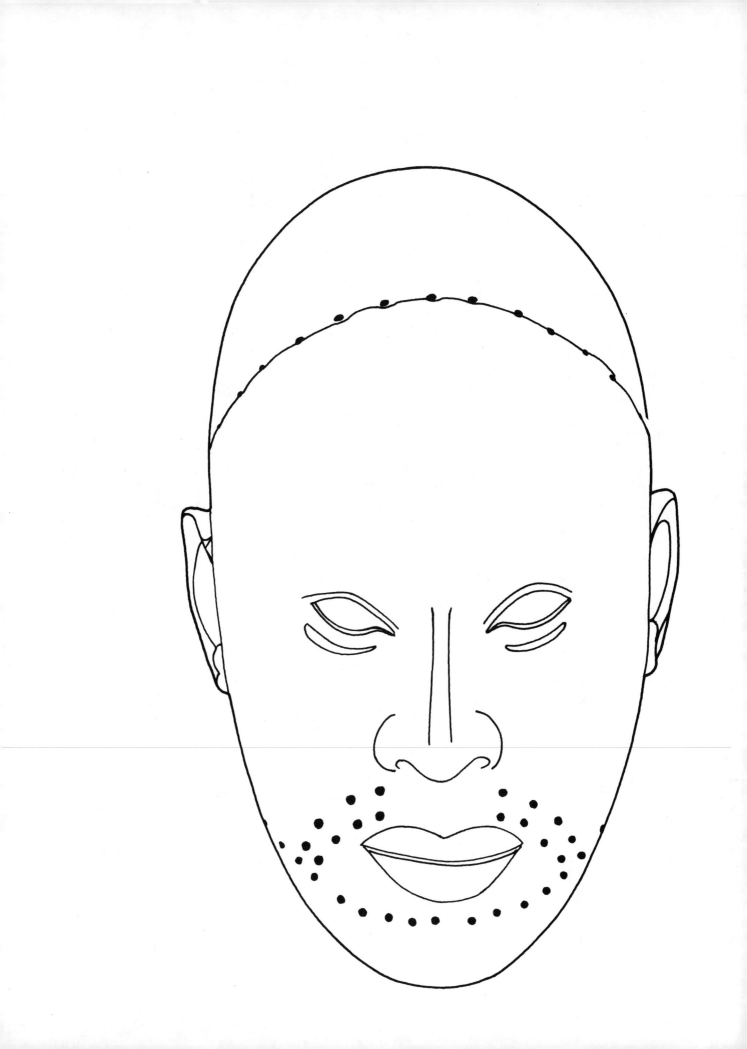

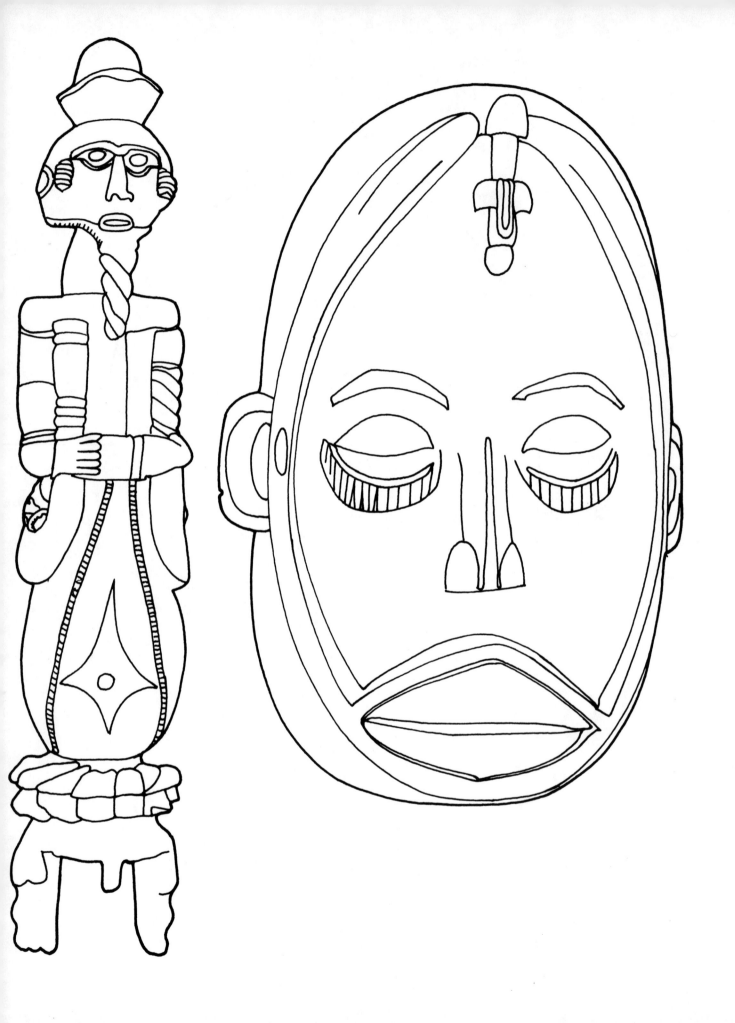

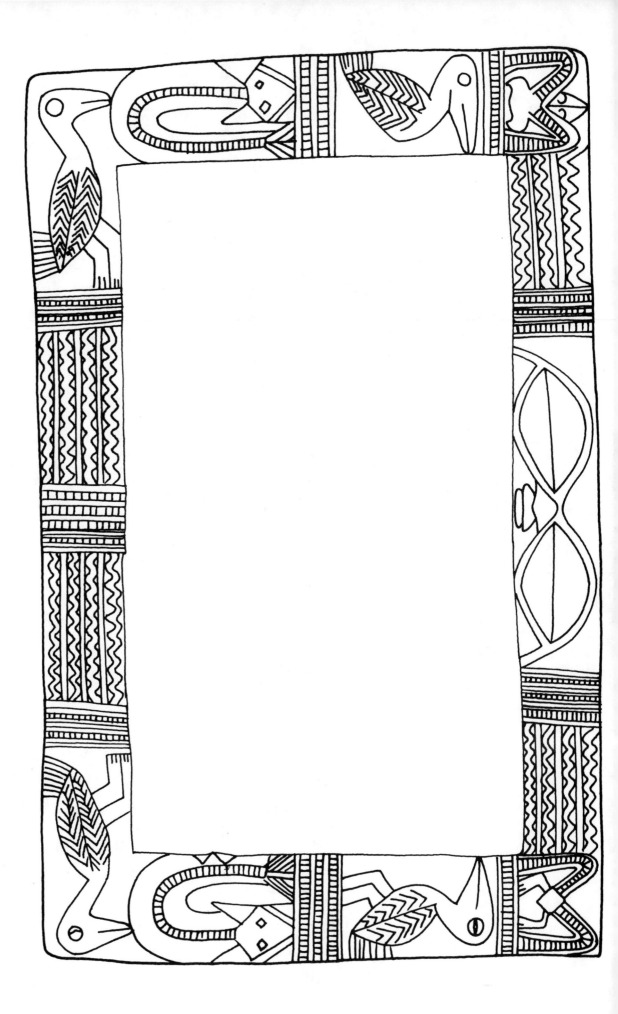

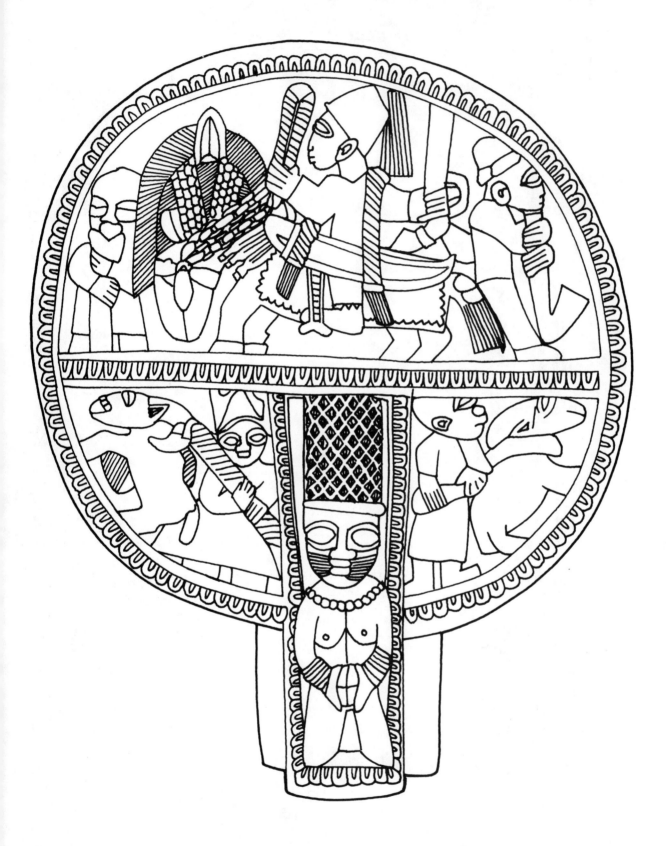

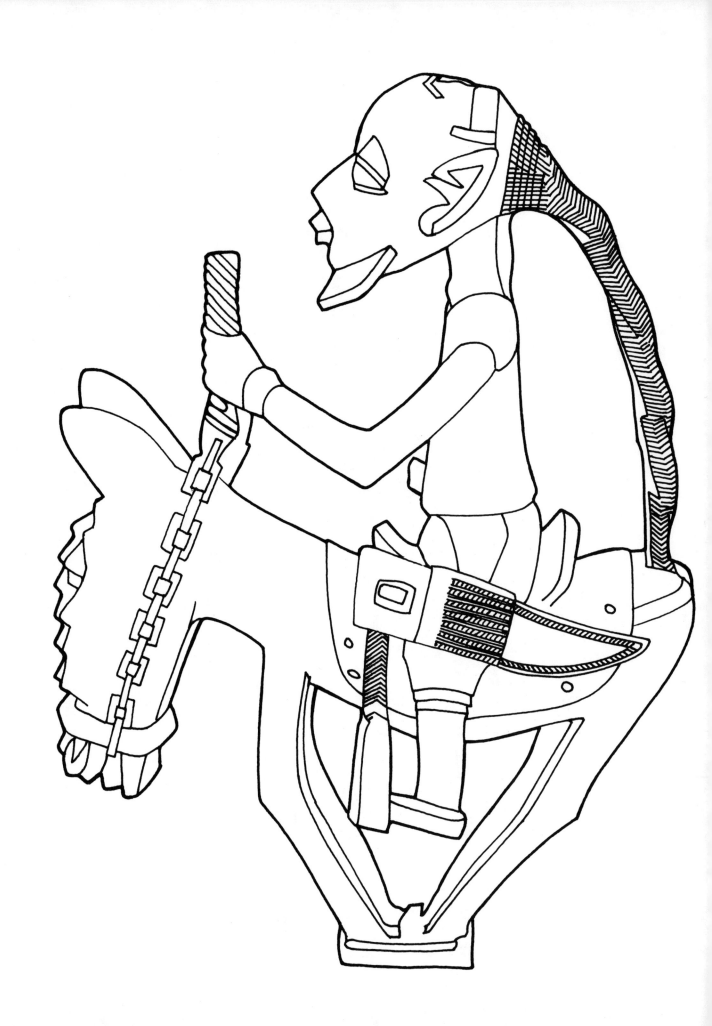

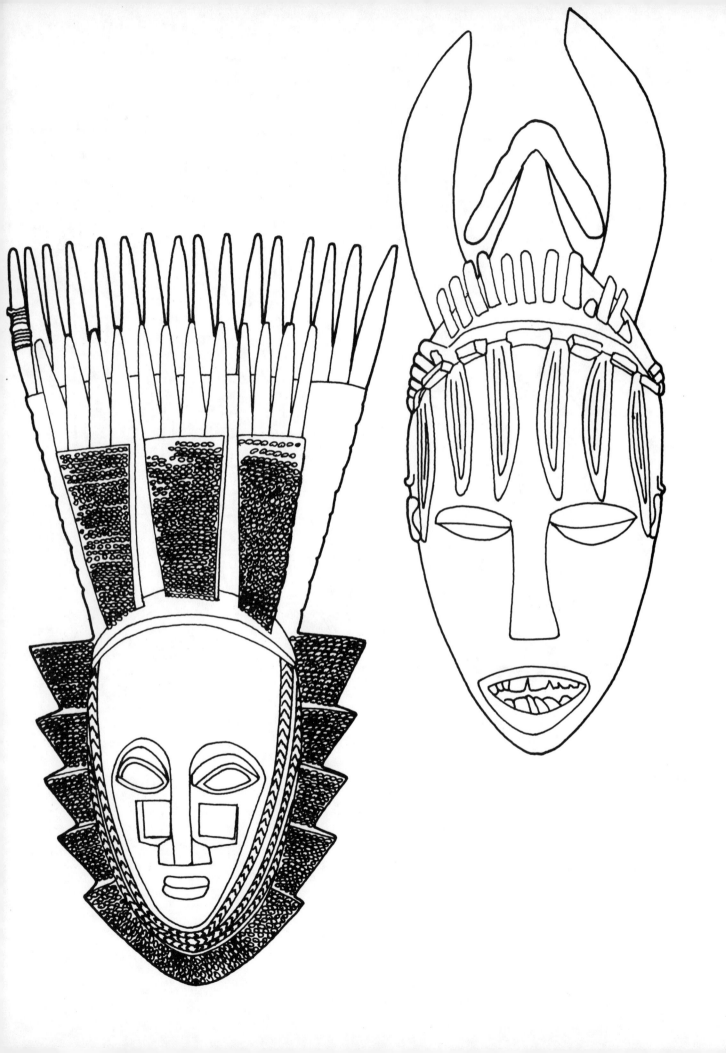

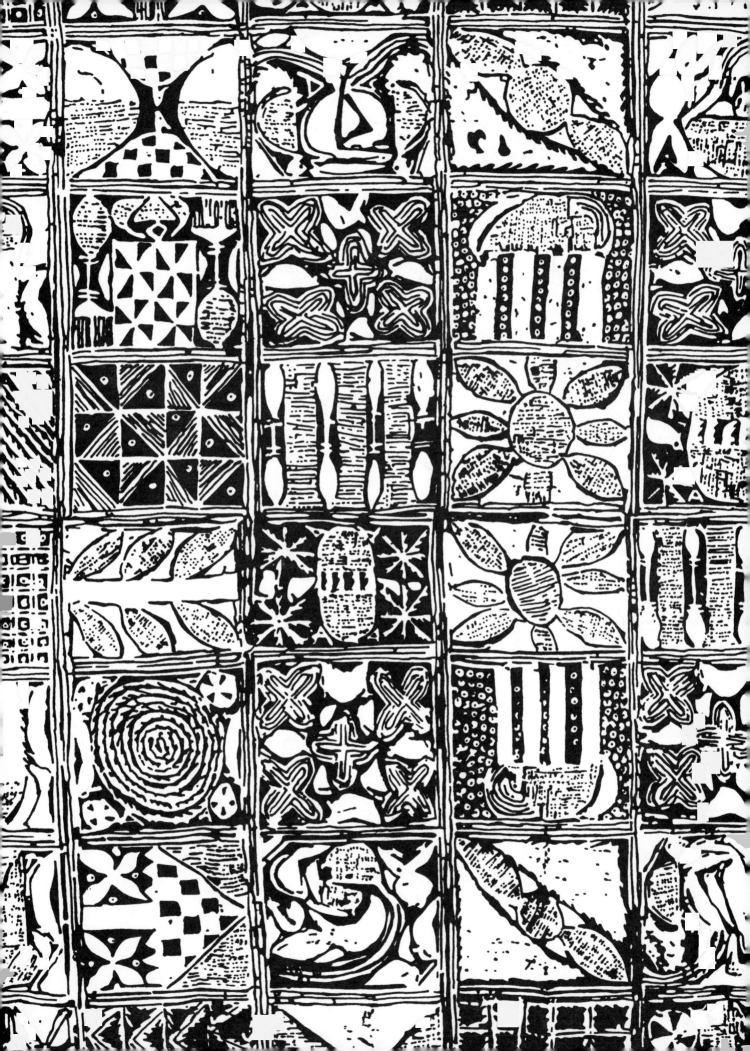

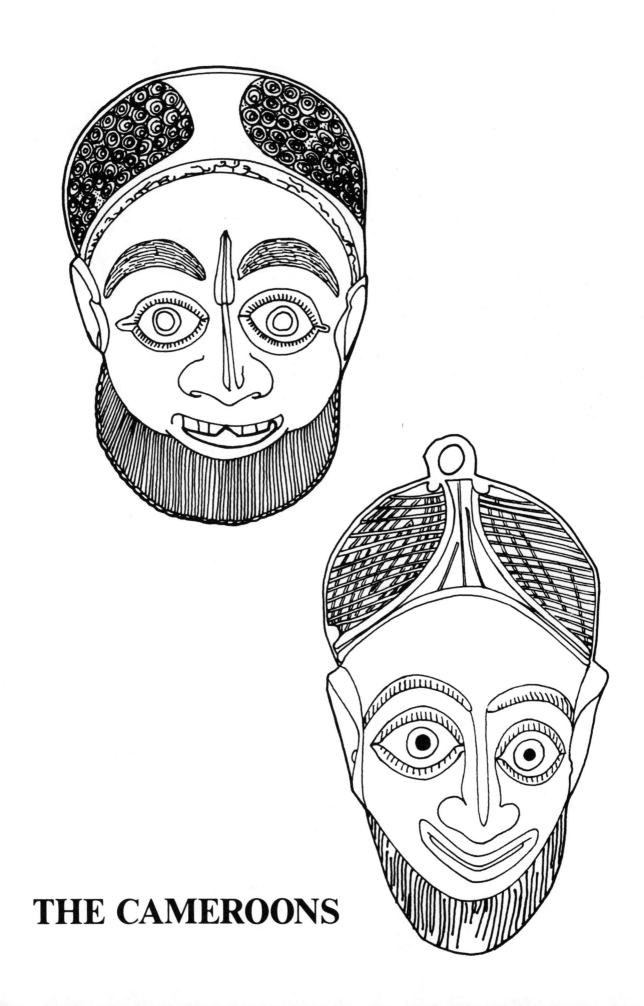

THE CAMEROONS

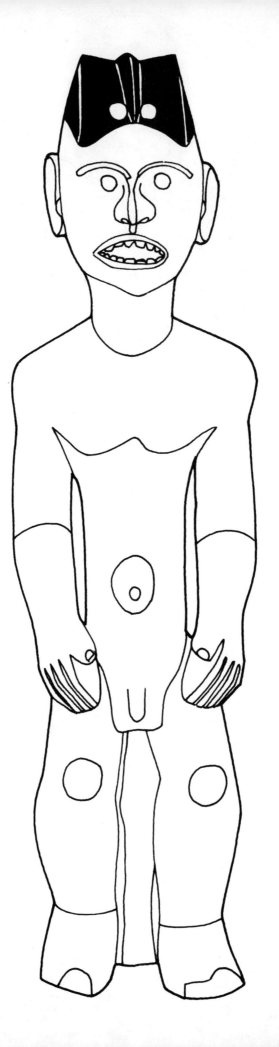

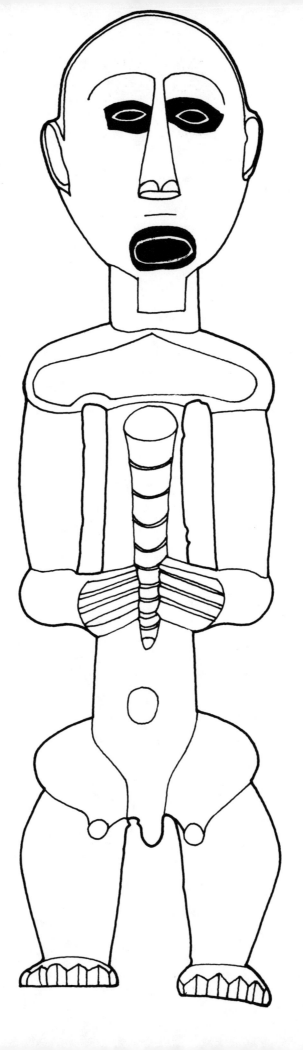

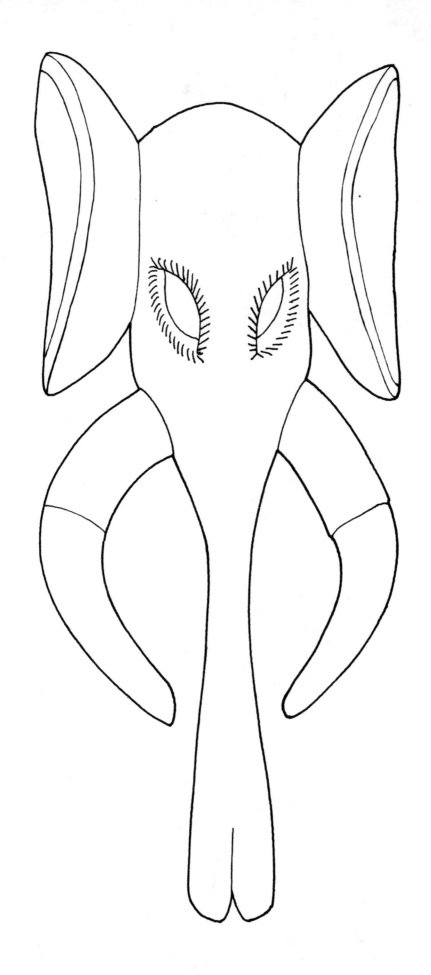

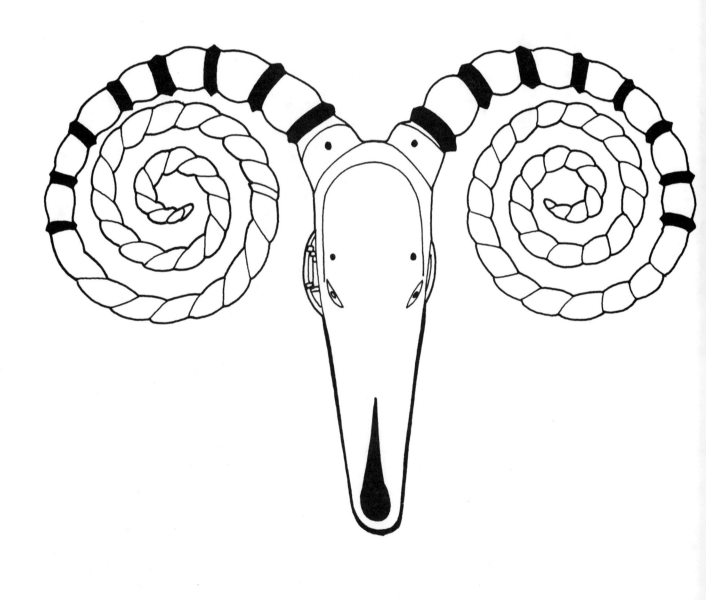

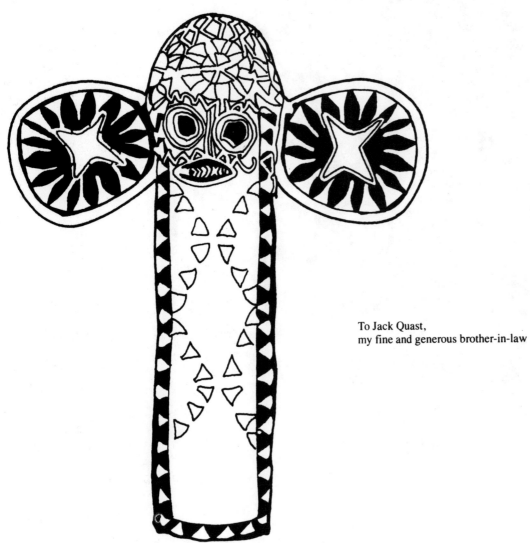

To Jack Quast,
my fine and generous brother-in-law

Colophon
Designed by Barbara Holdridge
Composed in Times Roman by Brown Composition, Baltimore,
    Maryland
Color separations by Capper, Inc., Knoxville, Tennessee
Printed on 75-pound Williamsburg Offset and bound by Worzalla
    Printers and Binders, Stevens Point, Wisconsin